Copyright © Bad Pup Projects 2016.
All rights reserved.
ISBN-10: 1541082303
ISBN-13: 978-1541082304

Poems of Du Fu
杜甫诗

Volume I
一册

An English-Chinese dual language book
英文中文双语言书

Edited by
编辑
Range Khan

Du Fu 杜甫

712–770 A.D.

Du Fu is widely regarded as one of the most notable poets not just of the Tang dynasty, but also one of the greatest poets of Chinese history. Known as the "Poet-Historian," Du Fu's poems give a rare cultural insight into the ancient lives of common folk and mandarins.

His poems are still read today and provide a wonderful introduction to Chinese poetry. This volume contains a selection of poems by Du Fu from 750-759 A.D.

Please note that the translations in this volume are not always literal. Some effort has been made to preserve the feel and meaning of the language, As well as the literal definitions of the words. We hope that readers will use the duallanguage format to gain a greater appreciation of the original 'sense' of the poems whilst being able to compare the different modes of expression in both English and Chinese.

We have used the simplified characters of modern China, as these are most relevant to current day usage. You may wish to study the traditional forms of these characters for increased historical accuracy.

Wagons of the Soldiers
750-751 A.D.

The wagons rumble and roll,
The horses whinny and neigh,
The infantry each have bows and arrows at their waists.
Their parents, wives and children come to see them off,
So much dust is stirred it hides the Xianyang bridge.
They tear clothes, stamp feet and, block the way, weeping
The weeping voices rise up and strike the clouds.
A passer-by at the roadside asks a conscript why.
The footman tells him drafts happen often.
"Some, at fifteen, were sent north to guard the river,
Even at forty, they were still in the west army fields
When we leave, the village chief binds our heads,
Returning here with heads white, we're sent back to the frontier.
At the border posts, shed blood becomes an ocean,
The martial emperor's ideas of expansion have no end.
You have not seen the two hundred districts of Han homes east of the mountains,
In a thousand villages and ten thousand hamlets, grow thorny trees.
Although there are strong women to grasp the hoe and the plough,
They grow some crops, but the fields have no order
Moreover, we soldiers of Qin withstand the bitterest fighting,
We're driven on like dogs and chickens.
Although an elder can ask me this,
How can a soldier dare to complain?
Even in this winter time,
Soldiers from west of the pass don't stop.
The magistrate is eager for taxes,
But how can we afford to pay?
We know it's true that having boys is bad,
While having girls is good;
Our girls can still be married to the neighbours,
Our sons are merely buried under a hundred grasses.
You have not seen on the border of Qinghai,
The ancient white skeletons no men gather?
The new ghosts are angered by injustice, the old ghosts weep,
Heaven's dark rains falls to dampen the voices' screeching."

兵车行
公元750-751年

车辚辚
马萧萧
行人弓箭各在腰
耶娘妻子走相送
尘埃不见咸阳桥
牵衣顿足阑道哭
哭声直上干云霄
道傍过者问行人
行人但云点行频
或从十五北防河
便至四十西营田
去时里正与裹头
归来头白还戍边
边亭流血成海水
武皇开边意未已
君不闻汉家山东二百州
千村万落生荆杞
纵有健妇把锄犁
禾生陇亩无东西
况复秦兵耐苦战
被驱不异犬与鸡
长者虽有问
役夫敢申恨
且如今年冬
未休关西卒
县官急索租
租税从何出
信知生男恶
反是生女好
生女犹得嫁比邻
生男埋没随百草
君不见青海头
古来白骨无人收
新鬼烦冤旧鬼哭
天阴雨湿声啾啾

Sighs of Autumn Rain: 1

754 AD

In autumn rain, the shoots rot and die,
Under the steps, the senna's colour is fresh.
Full green leaves fill the stems like a feather canopy,
Countless yellow flowers bloom like golden coins.
A cool wind moans and blows hard against you,
I fear that soon you'll find it hard to stand alone.
Upstairs the scholar lets down his white hair,
He faces the wind, breathes three scents, and weeps.

秋雨叹三首：一

公元754年

雨中百草秋烂死
阶下决明颜色鲜
著叶满枝翠羽盖
开花无数黄金钱
凉风萧萧吹汝急
恐汝后时难独立
堂上书生空白头
临风三嗅馨香泣

Sighs of Autumn Rain: 2

754 A.D.

Ceaseless wind and long rains swirl together this autumn,
Four seas and eight deserts all under a single cloud.
A horse going, an ox coming,
Can no longer be distinguished,
How now can muddy Jing and clear Wei be told apart?
The grain heads begin to grow, the millet's ears turn black,
Farmers and their wives get no news.
In the city, a bucket of rice costs a silken quilt,
Buyer and seller consider both of mutual worth.

秋雨叹三首：二

公元754年

阑风长雨秋纷纷
四海八荒同一云
去马来牛不复辨
浊泾清渭何当分
禾头生耳黍穗黑
农夫田妇无消息
城中斗米换衾绸
相许宁论两相直

Sighs of Autumn Rain: 3

754 A.D.

In Chang'an, who takes note of one in a cloth gown?
Locked behind the gate and watching the walls.
Old men don't go out, weeds grow tall,
Children without worry walk through wind and rain.
The rain's murmur hastens the early cold,
Bearded geese with wings wet find high flying hard.
Autumn gives had no sight of the white sun,
When will the mud dry into soil?

秋雨叹三首：三

公元754年

长安布衣谁比数
反锁衡门守环堵
老夫不出长蓬蒿
稚子无忧走风雨
雨声飕飕催早寒
胡雁翅湿高飞难
秋来未曾见白日
泥污后土何时干

Facing Snow

756 A.D.

From the battle cry many new ghosts,
Alone, worries and grieves an old father.
Chaotic clouds hang low at dusk,
Impatient snow dances back in the wind.
The ladle's cast aside, the cup without greens,
The stove remains a fiery red.
In many places, communications are broken,
In grief, I sit straight, my books empty.

对雪

公元756年

战哭多新鬼
愁吟独老翁
乱云低薄暮
急雪舞回风
瓢弃尊无绿
炉存火似红
数州消息断
愁坐正书空

In Abbot Zan's Room at Dayun Temple Four Poems: 1

757 A.D.

My heart is in a kingdom of splendid water,
My clothes are wet from this time of spring rains.
Through the gates I slowly walk,
The great court tranquil by design.
I reach the doors, they open and close again,
The bell rings, a vegetarian the meal is here.
Finest cream helps grow and expand our nature,
The diet gives support in my decline.
We've held together arm in arm so many days,
Opened our hearts without shame or evasion.
Golden orioles dart through the beams,
Purple doves descend from lattice screens.
I think my humble self has found a place to suit me,
By flowers I go at my own slow pace.
Tangxiu* raises me from sickness,
Smiles, asks me to write a poem.

*Tangxiu was a Buddhist monk and writer.

大云寺赞公房四首：一

公元757年

心在水精域
衣沾春雨时
洞门尽徐步
深院果幽期
到扉开复闭
撞钟斋及兹
醍醐长发性
饮食过扶衰
把臂有多日
开怀无愧辞
黄鹂度结构
紫鸽下罘罳
愚意会所适
花边行自迟
汤休起我病
微笑索题诗

In Abbot Zan's Room at Dayun Temple
Four Poems: 2

757 A.D.

Fine soft green silk shoes,
Shining bright white cotton scarves,
Kept deep in storage for the elders,
Fetched to use on my body.
My appearance changed, but without interest,
How can our friendship stay so fresh?
Daolin's talents do not age,
Huiyuan's* virtue surpasses men,
Rain pours at dusk; over the eaves and bamboo,
Wind blows through green celery at the well;
The sky is dark, a painting,
Most feel the damp dragon's scales.

---

*Daolin and Huiyuan were Buddhist monks in the fourth and fifth centuries.

大云寺赞公房四首：二

公元757年

细软青丝履
光明白氎巾
深藏供老宿
取用及吾身
自顾转无趣
交情何尚新
道林才不世
惠远德过人
雨泻暮檐竹
风吹青井芹
天阴对图画
最觉润龙鳞

In Abbot Zan's Room at Dayun Temple. Four Poems: 3

757 A.D.

The lamplight shines, I without sleep,
My heart clear, I smell the wonderful incense.
Deep in the night, the hall is suddenly lofty,
Wind stirs, gold clanks.
The black sky hides the springtime court,
In the pure earth hides a hidden fragrance.
The Jade Rope revolves and is severed,
The Iron Phoenix in the dark soars.*
Sanskrit sometimes flows out of the temple,
The lingering bells echo like thunder round my bed.
Tomorrow in the fertile field,
I'll bitterly behold the yellow dirt.

*The Jade Rope and Iron Phoenix are constellations.

大云寺赞公房四首：三

公元757年

灯影照无睡
心清闻妙香
夜深殿突兀
风动金银铛
天黑闭春院
地清栖暗芳
玉绳回断绝
铁凤森翱翔
梵放时出寺
钟残仍殷床
明朝在沃野
苦见尘沙黄

In Abbot Zan's Room at Dayun Temple. Four Poems: 4

757 A.D.

The boy draws from the well shining water,
He nimbly lifts the bucket to his hand.
He waters yet doesn't soak the earth,
And sweeps as if with no broom.
Bright rosy clouds again shine on the pavilion,
The clearing mist lifts high over the windows.
Leaning flowers cover over the path,
Dancing willows at the end of the steps.
The world's troublesome affairs compel me,
It's not yet the right time for retirement from the world
We meet, talk and agree deep in our hearts,
How can we always restrain our mouths?
I offer a goodbye and fetch my riding crop,
Parting for now, I turn my head at the last.
The vast expanse of mud defiles a man,
Listen to the many dogs across the land.
Although I am not get free from this yoke,
I sometimes come to rest from the clamour.
Around you, it's like white snow,
How can I be upset to grasp what's hot?

大云寺赞公房四首：四

公元757年

童儿汲井华
惯捷瓶上手
沾洒不濡地
扫除似无帚
明霞烂复阁
霁雾搴高牖
侧塞被径花
飘摇委墀柳
艰难世事迫
隐遁佳期后
晤语契深心
那能总箝口
奉辞还杖策
暂别终回首
泱泱泥污人
听听国多狗
既未免羁绊
时来憩奔走
近公如白雪
执热烦何有

Moonlit Night

756 A.D.

Tonight in Fuzhou, the moon,
In the women's chamber, one alone watches.
I pity the distant boy and girl,
They don't underwstand or remember Chang'an.
Her hair is wet in a fragrant cloud of mist,
In the moon's light, her arms appear as jade.
When shall we lean in the empty window,
Together in brightness, with tears dried?

月夜

公元757年

今夜鄜州月
闺中只独看
遥怜小儿女
未解忆长安
香雾云鬟湿
清辉玉臂寒
何时倚虚幌
双照泪痕干

Spring View

757 A.D.

The country is broken, hills and rivers remain,
City in spring, grass and trees are deep.
Moved by the moment, a flower's splashed with tears,
Regretting parting, a bird startles the heart.
The beacon fires have joined for three months,
Family letters are worth endless gold.
My white head I scratch, hair grows thinner,
And barely able now to hold a hairpin.

春望

公元757年

国破山河在
城春草木深
感时花溅泪
恨别鸟惊心
烽火连三月
家书抵万金
白头搔更短
浑欲不胜簪

Qiang Village: 1

757 A.D.

Towering red clouds in the west,
The sun sinks to the horizon.
A sparrow chirps on the wicker gate,
I return a traveller from a thousand miles.
My wife and children are surprised I'm here,
Shock calms and they wipe their tears.
Drifting through this disordered life,
By chance I have managed to return alive.
Neighbours fill the top of the wall,
They too sigh and sob.
Late at night we bring more candles,
And face each other as in a dream.

羌村：一

公元757年

西云赤云西
日脚下平地
柴门鸟雀噪
归客千里至
妻孥怪我在
惊定还拭泪
世乱遭飘荡
生还偶然遂
邻人满墙头
感叹亦歔欷
夜阑更秉烛
相对如梦寐

Qiang Village: 2

757 A.D.

Late in years, my life drags on,
Returning home, I find little joy.
My darling son will not leave my knee,
Fearing I will again go away.
Remember we used to seek the cool shade,
Among the trees beside the pool.
The whistling north wind is strong,
I worry of a hundred troubles.
At least I know the millet harvest's good,
Already I hear the grain press trickle.
For now I have enough to pour and drink,
I use it for brief comfort late in life.

羌村:二

公元757年

晚岁迫偷生
还家少欢趣
娇儿不离膝
畏我复却去
忆昔好追凉
故绕池边树
萧萧北风劲
抚事煎百虑
赖知禾黍收
已觉糟床注
如今足斟酌
且用慰迟暮

Qiang Village: 3

757 A.D.

The flock of chickens chaotically calls,
As guests arrive, the chickens fight.
I drive the chickens up into a tree,
Begin to hear a knock on the wicker gate.
Four or five elders,
Ask how long and far I have travelled.
In his hands , each carries something,
Pouring the wine jug, clouded combines with clear,
Bitterly resigned the wine's taste is thin,
There's nobody to farm the millet fields.
Conscription goes on without rest,
Children campaign further east.
I ask to sing for the elders,
In tribulation, I'm ashamed by deep feelings.
My song fnished, I face heaven and sigh,
Everyone present weeps freely.

羌村：三

公元757年

群鸡正乱叫
客至鸡斗争
驱鸡上树木
始闻叩柴荆
父老四五人
问我久远行
手中各有携
倾榼浊复清
苦辞酒味薄
黍地无人耕
兵革既未息
儿童尽东征
请为父老歌
艰难愧深情
歌罢仰天叹
四座泪纵横

Winding River: 1

758 A.D.

Each flower petal that flies lessens the spring,
In the wind float ten thousand drops to grieve a man.
I watch as the soon to be exhausted blossoms pass before my eyes,
Unsatiated by the much wine that enters my lips.
On the river, in the little hall nest Kingfishers,
By the flowered high tomb lies a unicorn
Invertigating the world, one must seek joy,
For what use would ephemeral reputation trip up this body?

曲江二首：一

公元758年

一片花飞减却春
风飘万点正愁人
且看欲尽花经眼
莫厌伤多酒入唇
江上小堂巢翡翠
花边高冢卧麒麟
细推物理须行乐
何用浮名绊此身

Winding River: 2

758 A.D.

I return from court each day and pawn spring clothing,
Every day to the river, drunk I return.
Debts for liquor most everywhere I go, I have
Living to seventy is always unusual.
Among the flowers, butterflies go deeper and deeper I see,
Amid water droplets, dragonflies leisurely fly.
Tales passing on the wind say time is always on the move,
So little time to know each other, we should not be apart.

曲江二首：二

公元758年

朝回日日典春衣
每日江头尽醉归
酒债寻常行处有
人生七十古来稀
穿花蛱蝶深深见
点水蜻蜓款款飞
传语风光共流转
暂时相赏莫相违

Spring Night in the Left Office

758 A.D.

Flowers hide in shadow of the palace wall at dusk,
Chirping birds depart to roost.
Stars overlooking ten thousand doors move,
The moon nears nine heavens or more.
Not sleeping, I hear a golden key;
Due to the wind, I think of jade pendants.
Tomorrow morning I have official matters,
Again and again, I ask about the night.

春宿左省

公元758年

花隐掖垣暮
啾啾栖鸟过
星临万户动
月傍九霄多
不寝听金钥
因风想玉珂
明朝有封事
数问夜如何

Clearing Rain

758 A.D.

Heaven's water has fallen, autumn clouds are thin,
From the west, ten thousand miles has blown the wind
This morning the land is a is good clear view,
Long rain has not harmed the farms.
A crammed row of willows shows hints of green,
On the hill, the pear's flowers are small and red.
A reed flute upstairs sounds,
A goose penetrates the high sky.

雨晴

公元758年

天水秋云薄
从西万里风
今朝好晴景
久雨不妨农
塞柳行疏翠
山梨结小红
胡笳楼上发
一雁入高空

Official at Stone Moat Village

759 A.D.

At dusk, I stopped at Stone Moat village,
There was an officer that night who captured men.
The old man escaped over the wall,
The old woman looked outside the door.
With what anger the officer shouted,
With what grief the woman cried.
I heard her send forth the words:
"Three boys in the Ye city garrison
One son sent a letter,
The other two have just died in battle.
The surviving son grips to live, for now,
The dead ones have met their final end.
Inside this house, there are no people left,
Only a grandson suckling on the breast.
The grandson's mother cannot go,
She comes and goes in an unfinished skirt.
Though an old woman with failing strength,
I ask you to take me with you tonight.
If you should need workers at Heyang,
To prepare your morning meal."
Her long speech died away into the night,
It seemed I heard her sob and whimper.
The sky brighteneed the road ahead,
Alone with the old man I leave.

石壕吏（陕县有石壕镇）

公元759年

暮投石壕村
有吏夜捉人
老翁逾墙走
老妇出门看
吏呼一何怒
妇啼一何苦
听妇前致词
三男邺城戍
一男附书至
二男新战死
存者且偷生
死者长已矣
室中更无人
惟有乳下孙
有孙母未去
出入无完裙
老妪力虽衰
请从吏夜归
急应河阳役
犹得备晨炊
夜久语声绝
如闻泣幽咽
天明登前途
独与老翁别

Written for Scholar Wei

759 A.D.

We've lived our lives and not seen each other,
Moved like the stars of Shen and Shang.*
What an evening is this evening,
Together sharing the light of this candle.
For how long can we stay young and strong?
Already we each have greying temples.
Visit old friends, half of them now ghosts,
Your exclamation brings heat to my gut.
We did not know it would be twenty years,
Before again gentleman would meet in your hall.
When we parted then, you were unmarried,
Suddenly boys and girls form a line.
Happy and content, they show respect to their father's friend,
Ask from which direction I come.
Even before the question has been answered,
The boys and girls begin to serve the wine.
In the night's rain, they cut spring chives,
Mix fresh cooked rice with golden millet.
My host says it's been hard for us to meet,
One cup now becomes ten cups.
After ten cups, still I am not drunk,
Intentionally drawing out out time.
Tomorrow we'll be separated by mountains,
Of worldly affairs, two indistinct in the vastness.

*Shen and Shang are two constellations which are never seen together.

赠卫八处士

公元759年

人生不相见
动如参与商
今夕复何夕
共此灯烛光
少壮能几时
鬓发各已苍
访旧半为鬼
惊呼热中肠
焉知二十载
重上君子堂
昔别君未婚
儿女忽成行
怡然敬父执
问我来何方
问答乃未已
驱儿罗酒浆
夜雨剪春韭
新炊间黄粱
主称会面难
一举累十觞
十觞亦不醉
感子故意长
明日隔山岳
世事两茫茫

Parting from Abbot Zan

759 A.D.

A hundred streams daily flow east,
The traveller goes on without rest.
My life is bitter, floating adrift,
What time will be the final end?
Abbot Zan, old among Buddhists,
Banished, came from the capital.
Still we're bothered by the earthly dust.
Reflected in our haggard expressions.
Willow twigs one morning in our hands;
Beans sprouted in the rain; ripe from then onward.
The body floats like a cloud,
Peace can be limited to south and north.
In a foreign land I meet an old friend,
With new happiness I can write my feelings.
The long is stoppered by the cold,
At year's end, hunger and chill pursue me.
Wild winds blow my travelling clothes,
I wish to depart toward the dusk blackness.
The horse neighs, remembering its old stable,
Returning birds have folded tired wings.
The places where we used to meet and part,
Shortly will be overgrown with thorns and brambles.
We look at each other, and see our old age;
Leaving or staying, we each must do our best.

别赞上人

公元759年

百川日东流
客去亦不息
我生苦漂荡
何时有终极
赞公释门老
放逐来上国
还为世尘婴
颇带憔悴色
杨枝晨在手
豆子雨已熟
是身如浮云
安可限南北
异县逢旧友
初忻写胸臆
天长关塞寒
岁暮饥冻逼
野风吹征衣
欲别向曛黑
马嘶思故枥
归鸟尽敛翼
古来聚散地
宿昔长荆棘
相看俱衰年
出处各努力

Staying Overnight with Abbot Zan

759 A.D.

How did your tin cane get here?
The autumn wind already soughs.
The rain's laid waste to the great court's chrysanthemums,
Frost has felled half the pond's lotuses.
Banished, you don't violate your nature,
In limbo, you don't depart from Chan.*
Now we've met, stay all night,
The Gansu** moon shines full-faced upon us.

*Chan is a form of Buddhism.
**Gansu is a province in the northwest of China.

宿赞公房

公元759年

杖锡何来此
秋风已飒然
雨荒深院菊
霜倒半池莲
放逐宁违性
虚空不离禅
相逢成夜宿
陇月向人圆

Taking Down a Trellis

759 A.D.

The sticks already tied wither and fall,
The pumpkin leaves become sparse.
It's lucky the white flowers already bloomed,
I peacefully let go of the green vines as they fade.
Sounds of autumn insects don't go,
What do the sparrows think at dusk?
Now, the world is one of cold and waste;
Human life has its beginning, too.

除架

公元759年

束薪已零落
瓠叶转萧疏
幸结白花了
宁辞青蔓除
秋虫声不去
暮雀意何如
寒事今牢落
人生亦有初

Thinking of Li Bai at the End of the Sky *

759 A.D.

Cold wind rises at the sky's end,
What thoughts occupy the gentleman's mind?
What time will thewild goose arrive?
The rivers and lakes are full of autumn water.
Literature and worldly success are opposed,
Demons exult in human failure.
Talk together with the hated poet,
Throw a poem into Miluo river.**

*Li Bai was was a friend and poet contemporary of Du Fu.

天末怀李白

公元759年

凉风起天末
君子意如何
鸿雁几时到
江湖秋水多
文章憎命达
魑魅喜人过
应共冤魂语
投诗赠汨罗

Thinking of My Brothers on a Moonlit Night

759 A.D.

Garrison drums cut off people's movements,
On the autumn border, a lone goose sounds.
Dew from tonight will be white,
The moon is as bright as in my homeland.
I have brothers dispersed throughout the land,
No home to ask if they are living or dead.
The letters we send never reached,
As still the soldiers do not rest.

月夜忆舍弟

公元759年

戍鼓断人行
边秋一雁声
露从今夜白
月是故乡明
有弟皆分散
无家问死生
寄书长不达
况乃未休兵

Printed in Great Britain
by Amazon